DOLOR

"DECEIVED BY LOVE"

DOLOR

"DECEIVED BY LOVE'"

By
Michael J. Stuckey Jr.

"Stuckey Publishing 2016"

Second Edition 2017
First Printing 2017

ISBN # 978-0-9986715-2-9

Stuckey Publishing
www.ArdentWriter.com

Previously published as; Dolor
Consisting of 49 poems.
Pub.: 09/24/2009 to end : 03/12/2013
ISBN: 978-1-4489-7957-8
(UN-Edited) by PUBLISHAMERICA, LLP

This Revised poetry manuscript is of the pain & the hope, one finds in romance.

Now known and titled as: Dolor; "Deceived By Love". Includes additional poems not previously published of poetry writings between the end of 2001 through 2003 containing the 84 Poems.

Michael said, " This collection of poetry was inspired by 2 past loves. Apparently Essence of Gray with a touch of Disease is me. By the end of this book, you will know of what I've learned, and what I would've gave several lifetimes without ever learning,.... Emotions!

Poetry Contents

CONTENTS

Hope We'll Last

I want to bring you inside
The house of love'
Walk beside the moon lit sky,
Penetrate the morning light.
I know what you've been dreaming of,
The words you long to hear,
The words I've longed to
Whisper in your ear.
Laugh and cry in this night
I know your deepest, darkest fears
Be with me till the lack of love
Parts its own way.

Just Opposing

Nothing matters but this moment,
the slow death of love,
as the perfume of Wild Roses
Ascends into the air.
Stripping my life,
Opposing my desire.

Romantic Distress

Of my heart, my mind runs rampant, thinking of
you.
When I gaze upon your eyes,
I wonder if you could be true.
I think of what could be,
What might not be.
For if I hesitate I could lose you,
For if I seize this moment, I stand to gain.
You and I, Dream or reality ?

My Beautiful Muffin

Not long ago, I said I didn't love you,
Don't want you, don't need you.
I lied, I am in love with you.
I want you, I need you,
You complete me.

Told you,
'You're in danger, you have to leave
I Can't lose another, lose you.'
Didn't even say goodbye.

Unfortunately it was true.
When you cried, It tore me apart.
I crumbled inside, as you walked out.
Just left, without even a fight.
Disappeared from my life,
Now I can't stop missing you.

Wanted to tell you then, as I am now,
Wanted to comfort you, to keep you for mine,
You really, truly fucked up my mind.

Time has past, I'm now free.
One day I will come look for thee,
For a chance, for us to be.
Lock me away in your prison,
Throw away the key,
So I'll never be free.

Where could you be.
I'm still in love with you, can't you see?
Impatiently waiting
Please come back, back to me.

Together

A tandem, a duet.
Pair of eyes, twist of twine.
Pair of morning doves,
The bubbling, crackling of champagne.
Clock hands,
Pair of laces.
You & me, a set of candles
Burning in the night.

The One

You're like an angel,
An Angel sent to me.
Inactivated by your style,
You've captured my heart, my mind.
When you look at me,
It takes my breath away.

I Need to know why,
I can't speak, when you're near me.
Is there a reason, a reason why,
I wanna be the one you call when you're lonely,
Be the one that drives you crazy,
Make you lose your mind in jealousy.

Need to know why,
Why you where sent to me,
My Angel. Tell me why,
What's the reason,
I wanna be the one you come home to,
The one you confide in,
Be whom you wake up to,
The one you share your heart and dreams with.

Please tell me, why I lose myself in your eyes.
Why can't I get you out of my mind.
You belong in the heavens, or by my side.
So please tell me why, what's the reason,
Tell me please, what did I do to deserve you?
What was it I said, that made you want me?
Tell me why you were sent to me?

You Unto Me

One summer evening saying goodbye,
Found myself saying hello.
Like a Fluntiena Orchid awaking,
Opening 'n' showing its beauty,
Striving to kiss the Moon's glow.

As you spoke to me.
Beside myself and Speechless,
Heart beating, thumping like a Rabbit's paw.
Desperately searching for Words to say,
Something, anything more.
Overwhelming thoughts of confusion,
Speechless, and now can not breathe.

It's depth I see in your eyes,
You're captivating.
Its Been moths, yet I remain,
Speechless and confused,
Gasping for air.

Thy only word, Hello.

Worth Breaking

From beginning to end, one thing remains true,
The way I feel about you.
Good times, bad times, Fighting, no longer talking,

The way you look at me,
The way I look at you.
from within each other's eyes,
Are thoughts, our demise,
Perhaps we should try,
Or should we not.

You wear this persona,
So many faces of so many shades,
I see through your disguise,
I know you better then you think.
Contemplations, complications.
As you penetrate through my walls,
As you know me better than most,
Please don't hide.

Thy heart, I wear on my sleeve,
No longer can I grieve.
The time is now,
Set aside your doubts, your fears,
Your contradicting mind,
It's only a moment in a lifetime.

Look in my eyes.
See the beginning to the end.
I will ask, then never speak of it again.

Unanswered

I gazed across a crowded room,
Saw the one within my dreams.
A lost love from another life,
A moment of passing thought, of another time.
Perhaps one to soon be mine.

I pondered a thought,
A way to forget her.
In my dreams we're together.
Another time, Another place,
In this dream I'm happy & safe.

As the dawn early rises, I feel despair.
Every new dawn brings more heartache & fear.
Is this love or simply infatuation?
Or am I a fool, for she is refined,
I wish she would be mine.

Is this infatuation?
A dream of a reality.
Is this a love, that is lost to me,
Please tell me, could we ever be?

I see her from time to time.
But I stand in silences.
Thoughts are always in my mind.
Why do you except things that shouldn't be,
When you could be with me.

Please don't. It's not worth crying,
I'll give you no reason, to shed a single tear,
Or have, weary of any fear.
I think of you as often, as my son.
For I must respect, accept things for what they are,
Watch the tears trickle, from your eyes.

Knowing we both know, you should be mine,
Though night brings an early dawn,
I lose patience in the day.
Perhaps time will soon be for you & me.
For now I will wait & bide My time.
When you're ready, and time is now.
Until the next time we meet, waiting I may be.

I've lost everything once,
Yet every thing I stand to gain.
We almost had a chance,
But neither of us were free.

So I await for your return,
For you to be free,
As it was, As it should be,
Soul mates You & Me.

Suspense

I stand here suitably within my self,
Wondering upon the moment we meet.
Suddenly realizing how we look,
May, may not, will indefinitely determine,
An outcome within an oblivion of time.

Will we gaze upon each other's eyes,
Curiously thinking,
For if it's possibility, will this be the one?
For if it's a friend, will it become a possibility?

No matter the outcome, I remain utterly within,
Curious, yet intrigued of thou's personality,
Impatiently in suspense,
Of the moment we meet again.

She Knows

Met this girl two years or so ago,
Friendships, girlfriends come and go.
She left me too.

Months went by,
No call and no visit, lost to me.
A constant thought, now a memory.

Unknown number,
An old friendship came back to me.
See each other time to time,
Of my dismay, I fear it's not enough,
She's always on my mind.

Talk about everything,
Tease each other in every way,
Comfort each other when need be.

She has a boyfriend 'n' happy as could be,
As which he is, I will never be.
As I for her, I'd do anything,
Anything for her, even stay away if need be.

While she reads, I hope she realizes,
knows what she means to me.
Our lost friendship came back.
So don't you see,
It's hope, Hope She brings me.

A Place In

When my friend came back to me.
I had said, 'It's hope, Hope you bring me.'

Lost a love, love of my life.
In reaction of:
Things involved in,
People involved with,
Being a half-breed,
Her father no longer approving.

Got divorced, and my world crumbled.
Now, her father is dying,
Liver cancer & brain tumors.
Once he's out of the way,
She may return to me.

So you see, you came back.
When the time is right, and time is now.
Perhaps my world will be complete.

We've been at peril, with enormous doubt,
You came back, with a gift of hope.
And you're the only one,who expected nothing,
Nothing in return.
For this you have a piece, of my heart,
A true friend, Thank you.

Love Letter

Your hand delicately brushes my hair,
My heart jumps as if chimes in the air,
Startling me so that I cling to you,
For fear of falling off a never-ending cliff.

The touch of your fingers grazing mine,
Delicate as a single drop of wine,
Rolling it around, I savor It on my tongue,
Try to make it last forever.

Like the beauty of a rose,
The words I'm falling, form in the sky and melt,
Your palm against my cheek,
Soft as the first winter's Snowflake.

Wait, I must catch my breath
It's your essence which may
be the death of me.

Cherish

Now and forever,
You are in my heart,
Till we die or depart.
For I love you today,
More than yesterday.
Now and forever you,
You have my Heart.

Chance

All the things now which stand true,
Leave me wondering about you.
Decision of a question to ask.

Found where I stand,
Don't know if I should be.
For if I ask, will it come true?
Or Disappointment?
I fear it'll hurt too.

Been there before, don't want it again.
If I hesitate, I stand to lose you.
Swallow my pride,
Thickheaded as can be,
Could you test the boundaries,
With your hand in mine?

Being Introduced

No watch can tell love's time, the hour is always.
Unfortunately it's always the right time,
Unbidden when least expected as now.
Joy only comes with infliction,
As a light craft darting across the sea,
When dropping anchor to stay.
Starts with, yet never finishing,
Sequence unredeemed.
During this moment of being,
Introduced to you.

Beauty

There is love in her eyes
The world is despised,
For she is filled with passion,
Though pain has arrived.
Through it all,
Love remains in Her eyes.

A Waiting Fool

The way you look at me,
The way you act,
The way you talk to me,
How can I not react?

At work Occasionally after,
Always the same.
Morning arrives, flip the script.
How it was is no longer how it is.
Sarcasm, short, direct, bitchy. Call is over.

Evening comes repeating itself.
Plans, dates never hold up.
Left disappointed, confused, irritated,
Why even set up?

I keep going back,
A Glutton for punishment.
Do I deserve it?
Maybe I should, maybe I shouldn't.
I can't take it anymore,
It'll never happen.
Being there for you,
Getting thrown aside, waiting.

Till time will know,
Repeating its self, flipping scripts,
Will it be, or will it be sorry?
Waiting as as a Fool.

A Call

I stand here in confusion,
Dreaming of the next time we meet,
For us to be together, not for the last time,
As one or as apart, but gather,
In my dreams we're together,
Hoping we'll become a reality.
Realizing there is nothing,
Except pain and suffering of a beautiful,
Adoring, intriguing memory.
Yet through it all,
Still, I await your call.

A Beginning

I left for home,
Not knowing when, or if I'll be back.
Took care of what I had to take care of,
Ran into an old girlfriend,
Nothing left, except to keep a promise,
To the one who caught my attention.

Before she asked,
I thought it would never be,
Then she said, she asked:
("promise me, you'll come back to me.
Promise, you won't leave me.
Promise me,
Promise me, you'll come back for me.")

At first I was not sure,
A promise in which might not be true.
Then saw the look in her eyes,

Upon thy last night, she asked, ('You promise')
My last night in the states,
I gave thee a set of pearls and a promise.
A kiss, not one but two she gave me,
Slow, soft, tasteful, our first kiss 11-26.

Anxious to go & come back,
For the holidays to be over,
To start something beautiful & new,
As well as a new year.
Resolution for this year, to be there,

From me to you, loyalty & devotion,
To help you find your state of divination,
A beginning with you, my promise I'll hold true.

By the Sea

Morning, I run with the sea,
Together we break,
On the white virgin sands.

Noon, Emerald flames leaping high,
Are quenched in moon's light.
Ember's barely stirring, into leaping fire.
Beautiful green fire in her eyes.
For I hope it's not me, whom she despises.

Night shy of mortality,
The sea a wild shout, gloomy dying out,
Orgasm of ecstasy, as smoldering remnants flying,
Humming, flying, humming.

Morning repeating itself,
I cry out, enchanted by the sea,
I wish I didn't have to flee.

Love Is Confusion

Wanting to love,
But there is too much pain.
Filled with confusion,
When love finally awaits.

Trivial

The last note of the song of the day,
She fades off, while staring at the flames.
My heart at peril, in leaping desires,
Rainbow colors fade from sight,
Come back to me,
On this night, as I write.

Once

I loved you once, a long time ago,
You stomped on my heart,
Toyed with my emotions.
It took a while, but finally, I got over you.

Now you've come back,
Expecting my love to have lasted.
You thought my arms would be open.
I turned from you, said, "goodbye."
You destroyed me once,
Won't give you another chance.

To my surprise,
You fell to your knees and cried,
Like an idiot, I took you back one more time.
Once again, and I don't know why.
A glutton for punishment,
Repeating each tear I've cried.

Now you wanna leave, taking everything,
That means something to me.
Tis the end of the day,
You're on your way.
Don't come back, I won't
Acknowledge you anyway.
Now & forever, I hate you,
You're Dead to me.

Getting Over

You're my everything,
You're trustful, honest,
Respecting, true to self.

You're nothing,
You're a bitch, overzealous, disrespectful,
Hypercritical, self righteous,
Lying, deceitful, backstabbing little whore.

I Can't stand you, can't stand being without you.
I need you, don't need you.
Want you, don't want anything to do with you.
Stopped thinking of you, can't forget you.
I Love you, no I hate you.
Wanna have a life with you, feel like killing you.
Don't wanna see your face, I see you everywhere

The smell of your perfume in every breeze,
Your voice makes me nauseous, no it settles the
rage inside.
Left drunk, high, used, abused,
Slipped, and spent, Getting over you
The hardest thing, I ever had to do.

September Moment

What once was could have been,
Though said, it will never be,
Misconceptions, dissolution, your truth is
hypocrisy.
Is it now a possibility?

What had been asked, granted!
What's asked now, will be accommodated
Your ability, loyalty, devotion, now questioned,
I remain curious.

Your heart & mind already defined,
Apart, souls meant to be,
may never linger, nor be hindered.
Leaves are turning, colder it's becoming.
Feelings of one now declared,
September's end, a confusing moment.

Dying Candle

Flowers dying,
Leaves becoming colorful.
A gentle breeze, as if a touch of a woman.
Days are short 'n' nights are long,
Glistening moon on a lake front.
Stars are wonderous, beautiful in sight.
This much I know is true,
None of this can hold a candle
To what I see, as I lose myself looking into you.

Rekindled

Full of ideas, hopes & dreams.
Is this an allusion, a false persona,
From which is your true self.

Both of us lay separate, yet as a pair,
Of green ember's, floating across the sea,
Desperately searching for land, as for each other.
Our search will come to an end,
The feeling of being complete,
When we're finally together.

Knowing this leaves me impatient to see land,
To hold you in my arms, to kiss you goodnight,
To sleep all day, wake up to you holding me tight.

To see the sparkle in your eyes,
The glow upon your face,
Our happiness would shine,
Like the lighthouse,
Off the coast of San Juan.

If this is an illusion, don't tell me the truth.
You steered up a feeling that was lost to me, you let
me loose.
Sorry I can't let you be, if you're my future,
I don't want to be free.

Contradiction

Smooth as silk, tacky as milk,
Lap her, slap her,
Playful, unconstrained,
Leave her, keep her,
Tasteful, plentiful,
To good, not good enough,
Tease me, bite me,
Beat me, use me,
Leave me alone,
Don't go.

A Pit Stop

Quick stop off at the Ville,
One longs to drink it all in,
But no time to lounge,
We must get onto gulp.
For the night is young,
With several pit stops along the way.
No bar is like the Ville,
Yet by the 3rd, we'll be stumbling.
No matter now, by the 5th we'll be sloshed,
Meeting the night's end.

Brunt of a Joke

Tell me to call you, no one's ever home,
Call your cell, no one there either,
Leave a message, though you never bother to call.
Tell me to come see you at work or after,
Then you treat me like just another customer.
Thought we were past that,
thought we had something.

Guess I'm the brunt of the joke,
that's not going to float.
If this were to continue,
I'll end up despising you.
Then I'll play with you,
When I'm done, I'll throw you aside,
Like an old pair of shoe's, and laugh as you cry.

When you ask why, I'll simply tell you,
Tis what you asked for,
hope you like the way it feels,
You're now the joke, go away.

One Night Stand

Rubber or raw, loose or tight,
Flexibility and thrusting with all our might,
Bleeding, screaming, kicked her out at the end of
the night.

Met her friend, went for a drink
But my aim was off, now blindly blinks.
Turned her around for another try.

Now I'm done, 'n' I had my fun,
Was going to send her on her way,
Then she said I'm bi,
Should I call a friend or leave anyway?

Unfortunately I had to have her again,
To get her friend, a body out of sight.
Something new, something nice, warm and tight,
I'll hit it again, later on tonight.

Self-deception

Allow me to introduce my self,
I am every body you see,
Your sister, your brother,
Father, mother, cousin,
Your friend, every stranger among you,
And even the ones you've never seen.

I am a man, or am I a woman
I wear thousands of thousands of faces,
From one moment to the next,
Never to reveal my true self.

You might break through one or two walls,
And look behind this mask of deception,
Only to find another.
You may find this unsettling or deceitful,
To me, Tis comfort, security of my heart.

I allowed one to see behind my masks,
To see who I really am,
Then she left 'n' took a piece of me,
Left pain in place.
To this day I've yet to see her again.

Until the day of my death,
where I will lay there with
A smile on my true face and arms wide open.

I bid you please do not try,
For I will only wear
These thousands of thousands of faces,
Never to allow the chance of emptiness,
Or for it to be filled with pain, again.

Fulfillment

Hear we are once again, bored my old friend,
You told me it was declared,
You're in the sights of the sniper.
Yet you lack the fulfillment of your convictions,
Your mouth wrote checks, your ass can't cash.
Time to pay: 1 knee, 5 fingers, and broken nose,
the first time.

Now the second time, gave you a smiley.
The serpent took your eyes,
You can no longer get high.
Used & abused, spent & toasted.
You offered your life to even up the score,
I took your daughter & made her a whore.
Video taped 'n' sent to you.

Now with my satisfaction, a thought to disappear.
I left you in your misery, hoping you'll die to.

My Distress

Morning,
Alarm goes off bringing depression,
Awoke again to see the sun,
Another miserable day, go to work.

Afternoon, get off of work,
Gratification, till we're both in pain.
Think I'd be happy, no bored, depressed,
Fighting with my self.

Night comes,
I awake energetic, rambunctious,
Nothing to do, no where to go,
Nothing on TV or on the radio.

Sun coming up, I try to sleep,
Nightmares, toss & turn, finally fall asleep.
Alarm goes off, awoke in my distress,
Realizing the events them selves, will only repeat.

Mystical

Long and gloomy night,
There's no stars out tonight.
Lights of the city shine real bright,
Sky too glows a iridescent blue.
Tomorrow will be a full moon,
Clear 'n' stars shining bright,
The black craft on a perfect night.

Capturing souls,
Letting spirit take flight.
All the goblins, ghouls, 'n' hobbits,
Running around enduring the night.
Pleasure of scaring and stealing life.

A moment in immortality,
Thoughts transpire leading to desire,
The witches, the warlocks, god of fire.
Realm of the mystical,
Held apart by a continuous line of time,
Which is penetrated through, opening your mind.

I'm Your Disease

Allow me to introduce myself,
I am the disease of your addiction.
You'll be driven to alcoholism,
Drugs, and eating disorders.
I am cunning, baffling and powerful.

That's me, I've killed millions 'n' enjoyed doing it,
I love to catch you by surprise,
I love pretending I'm your friend, and lover.
I've given you comfort.
Wasn't I there, when you were lonely,
When you wanted to die, didn't you call me.
I love to make you hurt 'n' make you cry,
Better yet, I love it when I make you so numb,
You can't hurt, you can't cry, you feel nothing at all.

I've given you complete satisfaction,
when you want it.
All I ask for in return, is long-term suffering.
I've always been there for you,
When things were going right, you invited me back.
You said you didn't deserve to be happy,
I agreed with you.
Together we were able to, to destroy your life.
I don't come uninvited, you choose to have me,
Instead of love and peace, many have chosen me.

I'm your disease,
For now I lay here quietly a waiting.
When you feel fully alive, I'll thrive and awaken.
Until we meet again,
I wish you continued suffering,
sweet nightmarish dreams, & death.

Death by Sanitarium

Welcome to a place where all stands still,
No one has ever left, and no one ever will.
This place where suicide is withheld,
Is where suicide is longed for.
Doctors sleeping with nurses,
Nurses sleeping with patient
Patient feeling empty as a shell.
For those who live subjected to repeat the day,
And for those of us who have died,
forced into purgatory,
Failed escape, yet we continue to try.
Welcome to the sanitarium,
You & I are now permanently confined.

Final Moment

This & that,
In & out,
Mental & emotional,
Masculinity & femininity,
Saint O' Masochism & Catholicism,
Line of tranquility, line of divinity,
Pain & suffering, happiness & bliss,
Somewhere I missed.
Arms wide open, smile on my face,
Never finished in its place.
long as I have a want,
I have a reason for living,
Satisfaction is my death.

Day Dreams

I dream of a life,
Without pain and sickness.
Yet I live a life of hell,
I my day dreams I am well.
No longer will I seek inside,
For dreams of being well,
For I can only find a life of living hell.

Within My Sleep

In my sleep, there are no dreams,
In my sleep, I hear no screams,
In my sleep, I feel death inside,
In my sleep, I'm happily confined.

Conflict-ion

Rejoining at water's edge,
my misconception 'n' illusions.
The cold of the spray, being stripped away,
as if it's me, crashing against the rocks.
Tearing apart like green diamonds of the salty sea.
Leaping, lunging overhead,
Softly rejoining as I sit 'n' stir,
waiting to be whole once again.

I Am ?

Once told, repetitively lived.
Tormented, distraught, emotionally torn apart.
Aging soul, body decaying, intelligence sound.
Unable to look away, unable to forget,
Everyone in the family lives, I go nowhere.
Physically broken, I keep note,
Visually, mentally, everything in its time & date,
Conversations of past & current,
Seems what once was, still is,
Everyone else passes on, I remain,
Different religions, different names,
I'm called, I am, the Warrior.

Essence of Gray

Twisted thoughts, a soul's disease,
Divinity / tranquility, painful pleasures are these,
Month long only a glimmer in time,
Divination & true love, all within the same lie.

Solace

Like any other moment,
My life is filled with deception,
Emotional misery, sorrow, & regret,
For I awoke yet again, longing for thy end.

Desperately grasping for something,
anything to feel.
Razors edge, that stinging burn as I cut into my
skin, I feel again.
Now in my solace, I am comfortable,
My scars I were inside, you can not see them.
In the blood, the blood I thrive once more.

Maybe this will be the day they come for me,
Tearing away my skin, releasing me from these,
bonds of mortality.

Typical

Friend & family, one in the same.
Lies today, deception tomorrow,
Betrayal yesterday.
Loyalty lost, devotion a myth,
Disappointment comes,
Within every morning's mist.

Convicted

Bored out of my mind
This job's like doing time.
Blow job for gas, like cig's for ass.

6 am, ramen noodles, cookies & chips,
In garbage bag, an hour latter,
Smells alright, just enough to fill me up tonight.

10 pm, lock down.
No money, no treats. A biscuit would be nice.
Gas station to population, 2 week stay,
At last, a vacation.

Becoming

U say maybe, you're driving me crazy.
I'll be indecisive, you'll be happy.
Lies you've told me, friends you claim them to be.
Indebted to me now, this illusions clearing.

Coming home, you're being a disloyal, lying,
Self-righteous, little fuck again.

Like nitroglycerin, I'm becoming.
Shake me, drop me, throw me,
Unstable you've made me.
Your debt of deception, I've come to collect.

Coming home, you're being a disloyal, lying,
Self-righteous, little fuck, again.

With your love never shown to me,
Justification is mine, I'll cut you into pieces,
Drink of your essence, capturing your soul,
My slave you'll be, for eternity.

Some Acknowledgment

Right when I needed you the most,
You left me standing there alone.
Now I'm at the end of my rope,
And you're living, as you were.
Running around night after night,
While I'm banging, my head against the floor…

You say, "It'll be all right,
Just give yourself time to heal,
Just work through what you feel."

Now I see you everywhere,
Doing all the things we used to do,
Can't stop thinking about you,
The smell of your perfume 'n' sound of your voice,
It's driving me insane.
The way you look at me cuts me like a knife,
Why don't you add a little salt, for good measure,
For some acknowledgment.

Just when I can't take any more,
I can almost hear you say, "It'll be all right,
Just give yourself time to heal,
Just work through what you feel."

Now here you are,
You showed up at my door, looking for some ass,
Make up, then he comes & picks you up.
And I'm right back where I started before,
Banging my head against the floor.

You said you don't know him, that was just a lie,
He's supposed to be our best friend,
He used to come over and get high,
With you right by my side, now I feel I wanna die.

Please don't pay me any mind,
Just let the rope tighten up. It's hanging right
outside.
My feelings I can't hide,
Swinging by a Colombian necktie.
So my blood is on your hands,
Now you see what it is to cry.

Come to my grave you'll hear my voice,
Like the wind telling you, "It'll be all right,
Just give yourself time to heal,
Work through what you feel."

But the rope broke,
The knife was to dull.
This OD isn't working,
You're banging on my door, woke me up.
Bag & gag you, while I kill our best friend.
Maybe then, the pain will subside.
Maybe in time, let me know you're still mine.
I'll love you, till the end of time.

To Have

Wrong places led,
For I couldn't be bound.
At first not, but your moment is now,
then I will live.

What you were, the one,
No matter how I weigh it,
You're destined to go.

In the Seat,
'Tis simplistic to be the one,
Like that sparkle falling away,
Think it'll sinkin, anyway.

You I Dream

Nights light blinded sight,
Chains that bind,
This bleeding heart of mine.
Cocoon wrapped tight,
Dream in a nun-silent night.
Truculent experience's bound to you,
Black Veil I'll stay true.
My dreams like auto-erotic asphyxiation.

Asked

Thousand stories, one look on a face.
Nor deceiver, nor lie,
told look in a pair of eyes.
Prominent discussion, glorious,
or tragic outcome,
Insurmountable odds,
prominently asked question,
Will You Marry Me.?

With Me

As a child daydreams
Left me captivated by you.
REM sleep, we're together.
Through many of years,
Things we've done together.
To each other, for each other,
Never have you physically been here.
Together we've surpassed all my fantasies.

No matter how dark, demented,
Sadistic, violent or romantic,
Never have I lied to you.
I've shared every part of myself,
Seen every side of you.
The one constant,
One truth throughout my life.

Over decades that have gone by,
You slipped away from me.
Unkind as the years may have been,
You have never been here,
Yet you've always been there.

Blurry image, foot of my bed
Beckoning me, a voice so familiar.
An incredible love filled me.
Beside me, image clearer.
You haven't changed in all these years.
Overcome with teary eyes,
You've come back to me,

"I've never left." you replied.
Another chance, our secret love affair.

Be My

you laid this day, embraced in my arms,
same as the last, hopefully the next.
Each moment felt as if the first time.
Yet to get bored, yet to be ignored.
a king to you, as my queen to me.
Confucius has never known, what's known to me,
Valentine, will you be mine, oh Valentine?

Endless Light

Shimmering golden wheat field
Of brown highlighted, blond hair.
Young soul, baring through
Brilliant intrinsic brown eyes.
Words spoken softly, from behind luscious lips
As if whispers, carried in a gentle breeze.
Flawless lines, shown in each graceful movement.
Every glance, within every expression.
Little secrets being told.
Exposing different sides 'n' the essence of
Delicate personality.
Separate moments witnessed,
Strung together in thought,
Reflecting that of a breathtaking symphony.

Secret 1

Days, and woman, like seasons, have come & gone.
Bequeath the thought of thy still beating heart.
The smell of your skin is more enticing
Than all the flowers in a floral shop.
Thy complacency boggles your mind,
Your emotions confuse me all the time,
Secret 1, of our affair.

Reveled

Your body's bliss, only known to me.
Thy soul, I take as thy servant in the afterlife.
In the neurotic, thy erotic pleasures steadily wilts
The consuming rush at the moment of your death.
I bask only when your mutilated corps,
lies upon my feet.
It's then I scratch the surface of becoming
Momentarily empowered and I thrive as your god.

Progression

I once was wild, searching for that moment of bliss.
Brought back from the darkness, of divination.
Painfully overwhelming,
Pulled apart by emotions I've never known.
Choking with unshared tears, grasping at me.
At worst, exposing my only fear.
Though the days are sunny and filled with promise
Gloomy is my outlook,
for domesticated I've become.
A life I should've lived from the start.
Second guessing what came naturally
Each emotion amplified,
yet remaining with no guilt.
My own shame, I only have myself to blame.
Evolved to decrepit & slightly insane,
Grateful for the new chance I've been given.
Proud of Thy new achievements.
This life I've come back to,
This life I have gained is slowly killing me.

Nightstand

Meet someone new, just so I can feel,
My nature is without compassion.
Ravish your body, as you abuse mine.
Thou caged within, lose myself when inside of you.
Disgusted I am when looking at you.
A few more hours, then a shower
Scrub away the remnants of you.
She left on the nightstand, note & money
Thanks for the good time I'll call again.

Your Puppet

Spend my time, monotony of daily routine,
Empty & numb to all that's around me.
Asleep I seem to be, longing to awake
From this empty existence.
This life without you is killing me.

Phone rings. Find myself wishing it was you.
Smell your perfume. Eagerly I look around for you
Hearing your voice rekindles a torch,
When finally I see you,
Bursting with things to say.
Crucial moment & it comes out all the wrong way.
Hold you in my arms again, the void dissipates,
I fear I'm falling, falling in love with you

Elaboration of comment

Though my mind is clouded with judgment,
My heart seemingly misled,
it's you I see clearly, for you are my Muse.

Hear your Screams

Before time 'n' during life,
Of who you've been.
Evolution evolves in place,
Woman you're becoming.
As worlds revolve,
Like a Zahra, from yearling to stem,
To birth of a bud, in it's own beauty of grace.
Opening, showing all its beauty.
Beckoning our Souls,
Releasing its gift of life to all around.
Across lingering time,
We each & all belong to one-another.
Thou apart, relying on involvements,
Screaming, I don't want false promises.

Becoming Vintage

I was once as a seed, planted,
Nourished, for months.
Flourished leafed vine, I had become.
As flowers bloomed,
Grapes of my vines, harvested 1977.
Year of my birth,
Pressed & drummed, aged 7 years,
Poured into 6 meticulous bottles,
Only type of its kind.
A single bottle burst,
5 bottles, crated & shelved.
Slightly imperfect, my value grew.

Moved around & sheltered,
Another broken, by a clumsy oaf.
4 survived 'n' slightly tarnished,
Allowed to marinate, my year of aging, 21.
My crate was sold to a collector.
Yet another bottle broken,
3 imperfect bottles remain.
2000 aged now 23 years.
Scars of my body,
That of scratches on my bottles.
My labels are perfect,
As is my contents: bold, wet, sweat
With a full bite, an exploding flavor.
Just that much more alluring.
Well on my way of becoming,
An exquisite Vintage Wine.

Lunch Between Us

Glistening fingers,
Juices dripping off chin.
Like kings of the past,
Smiling foolishly.
Glutton, I will always be,
For Mi Chica can only satisfy me.

No More Sunshine

Clouds of gray seeping through.
Peril, where my heart once lay.
Angst, where temptation prevailed.
Awakened to the lack of love parting its own way.
Questions holding no answers.
Spoken words, bearing no weight.
Your love not forgotten,
In a mist of a dark nothingness,
Millions of thoughts, all I can say,
I've missed you.

Existential Life

Disappointing and monstrous,
To find they brought me back.
Physical and emotional suffering, intensified.
Caught up in day dreams of
Goals and achievements.
For I now have a ten year plan
My fantasy is full of a life,
I was never given the chance to live.
Dreams with in my sleep,
Continuous, excruciating reminder,
Of the life I lived, before I awoke.
Conflict and regret is life's travesty,
In the eyes of thy own reflection.
Filled with confusion when trying
To navigate through this life of normalcy.
The life I come from,
makes the life I now have seem all wrong.

Poetic Romance

Like an entangled web,
Each word forms sinful pleasures.
Blackened blood coursing through
Veins of thy broken heart.
Drowning in a sea of unfulfilled promises,
Eagerly consuming the taste of you,
just for a little piece of heaven,
Entrapped by your virtue, I turn from you.
Hope-filled indiscretions
keep me chasing after you.
I turn away, fighting my own desires,
To deal with the knowledge, of this poetic romance.
You come back with a burning written intentions.
Not only I have shown interest.

Entranced

Exquisite specimen on the,
Verge of extinction.
Enticing, though conservative.
Boisterous when tended to,
Boldly standing alone,
Offering a supported spleen.

Neither intrusive nor overbearing.
Beauty unmatched,
Possessing a fragrance of woe.
Like no other, perfect you were made,
Remarkable woman you're becoming.

What If

What If I was right
& no person, nor words,
Could make me wrong,
Or convince you, you didn't belong?
What If you followed your heart?
You wanted to be by my side.
What if you are most important, in my life?
You became a woman, then a wife,
Now a mother, dream house & no regrets.
What if we where the same creed,
origin, or nationality?
What If you weren't scared?

All I Want

All I want is someone,
to walk this journey of life with.
Someone to be loyal and devoted.
Someone to be honest and true.

All I want is someone,
to walk this journey of life with.
Someone to be affectionate & sensual.
Someone to be intelligent & breathtakingly
beautiful.

All I want is someone,
to walk this journey of life with.
Someone to be sarcastically bitchy.
Someone to be erotic and seductive.
Someone to enjoy the pleasures of infliction with.

All I want is someone,
to walk this journey of life with.
Someone to be from the old country,
with old country beliefs.
Someone to know what it is to be a Woman.
Someone to never give me a reason to not trust her.
Someone to be about & have a family with.
Someone to grow old with.

All I want is to know what it is to be loved,
as I have loved others.

A Man's Woe

Out of nowhere,
She appeared, sensual 'n' erotic.
Her very smell was of an aphrodisiac.
Expressive way of a bitchy attitude,
slightly neurotic.
Very essence, an infection, poison to one's soul.
Unable to break free, continually hard up for,
Simply, a glutton for more.
Wooed I was, a relationship it became.
Friends comments hindered,
Abrupt ending, manipulated, and scared.
I am only to blame.
For I fear I will never be the same.

Virtuous

You try to make things the way
You think they oughta be.
Never realizing you are all I see,
Not just a physical gratification,
Shoulder to shoulder metaphorically by my side.
Never to let you fall behind.
Tears entice thous around you,
Be yourself & forget their faults.
Knowing no better of what they do,
No longer should you except punishment.
Their ignorance 'n' arrogance is to blame.
While your account of deeds
Guides you to Jannah.
Judgment they will all too soon have.
A comfort this may not hold,
Your dreams are bold in a way no one knows.
Chemical words to an enraging inferno,
A hurtful lie, I'll never tell you.

Goth

Lives in shadows,
With black cloud overhead.
Haunted by her own inner demons.
Consumed by her conflicted heart.
Bound by family convictions.
The way of her, believed to be full of sin.
Heart leads, as she wades through life.
An intriguing woman,
Not meant for this time,
For this harsh world.
She's a child of the dawn's light,
An unnoticed Princess.

Yes, that's me

Look and you'll see
My hair short & stubby
My eyes dark as night sky
My arm's strong embrace
My hands worked raw
My heart lay broken
I'm the shoulder you lean on
I never let you down
My friends, I'm your security
I live for no conceivable reason
I hope to find love returned one day
I dream Gilded poems written in blood
It's all clear as can be.
That's positively, absolutely, me.

Hey Girl

Love that Girl,
Like a stallion loves to run free.
I said I love that Girl,
Like a stallion loves to run free.
Love to call her in the morning,
Love to call her,
"Hey there, Girl!"

Of Sustenance

This is the poem, that of ages.
In the loss of moon's light,
That pulls & tears,
Because essence of words felt.
Because temptation burns deep within.
And when pleasure overwhelms you,
fear takes over,
This is the poem that endue wisps,
That can't be bound nor given.

Sight

Black night sky,
Bottom depths of the sea,
Rose flavored La-Rue,
Blood, coursing through one's veins.
Darkness, of one's eternal soul.
Intentions, only I know,
Solace in daring times.

Of Dana's Light

Your words devout speak full of heart.
Gasping as my breath escapes me, a tear apart.
Intrigued yet speechless, never more enticing.
Thy aspirations 'n' beauty, of louder words,
Only an image of such innocents, never spoken,
My muse could portray.

Yearning For

Sensual expression,
Leaving, blinded sight.
Void dissipates, affection of hope.
Lost words of secret whispers,
Through luscious lips.
Alluring imperfection,
Of a bleeding heart's embrace.

Dear Chica

I would like to tell you,
I'm really into you.
You tell me, Let's take it slow.
You tell me, You're scared.
You tell me, I've been hurt before.
I would like to tell you,
My heart skips, and I feel alive,
So during our next encounter, allow me to thrive,
To hear the voice, to see the face,
Of this beauty, I wished was by my side.

A Lords Muse

Look and you'll see,
Eyes of death, dark as night sky.
Arm's strong embrace, with nothing to protect.
Heart lay empty 'n' frozen, to everyone around.
Still alive, for a reason yet to be found.
Of Nobility, dreaming gilded poems.
It's all clear as can be,
Once free, now emotionally captivated of thee.
Her pain, expressing that of thy own secrets.
Her spirit, only to rival my own.
Thy deprived ambitions, only she could understand.
Thriving urge, to write for her,
Yearning, to write to her.
Con-tenants apart, with a picture, once given.
Expression upon her face, dreams within her eyes.
Gothic princesses heart, told in her lyrics of mind.
Hanging on each syllable, I have forgotten time.
Lost in her words, that of a heavy weight,
Breaking the cold block within thy chest.
Enticed by each line unfolding,
Engulfed by the story she's telling,
She's becoming the muse of thy own writings,
Longing to be of whom her poems are written.
A lord I am, spelled I should not be,
Of a poet, a woman, a princess I've never met.

Moment's Desire

With a young, eager way, she walks past.
Bounce in her step, as she turns, throws her long
black curly hair back.
Glance over her shoulder, bashful smile of
innocents as she leaves waving,
I watch, toned long legs, nice ass, and defined back
line, has me reeling.
A moment goes by, she returns, in thralls, eager i
am to her approach.
Wanting a taste of her lips, i hold off.
She leaves my sight again, disappointed i am,
For i have yet to speak.

Begin my journey to vacate the place.
She walks up to me with an undeniable presence,
Stupendous full breast, licking her luscious lips,
Slightly turns away with a bright smile.
Fragrance of her is enticing,
A hunger grows only she can quench,
I step in and up to. She stops,
Looks up as it's hard to walk,
I hand her my card, "Look me up."
She replies, "I will,'" Turns and walks away,
ecstatic and uplifted.

I turn away, as i re-situate myself,
And notice a biker nodding to me.
Home again, awaiting her message,
Longing the mutual desires to be satisfied.

To Marry

Tis thou Lady whom honors,
Carrying on thous last name.
Tis thy Privilege to have the honor,
An obligation of loyalty,
Promise to never allow thy lady,
To diminish her stature of queen,
Nor compromise thou heart, with mind.
For anything beneath,
thy lady's inherited act of nobility.

Do you know it's over?

What look could be ignored, where each expression
holds such power to hurt.
What action could be forgiven, when only the
finality of infliction is all we notice.
What words could justify,
who has loss of ones heart.

When confliction of emotions has you in tears.
When infliction of thoughts,
has you plotting payback.
When an unbearable ache within your chest, has
you hiding from everything.
When destruction of your world,
has left you reeling inside yourself.

Curled up in the corner, beneath the rainy shower.
No little foot steps, trampling across the floor.
Sound of hollowed echoes stir through the house.
Old, cold, bitter, alone, plagued by regret,
When you realize, you have allowed all of this.
Still longing for that moment of love returned.

ABOUT THE AUTHOR

Born in the summer of 1977, Michael began writing emotionally torturous writing's & poetry as a child. He spent 19 long yrs in Tile & Stone becoming a master stones-man and installer, then forced to retire from the exceptional career he had built in 2008. Since that time, Michael became a Published Author / Writer of several Poetry books, recipe books, songs, and realistic thriller fiction novels.

Main website: www.ArdentWriter.com

www.ingramcontent.com/pod-product-compliance
Lightning Source LLC
Chambersburg PA
CBHW051901090426
42811CB00003B/415